What is Pediatric Occupational Therapy?

Occupational therapists (OTs) work with children with a variety of diagnoses including, but not limited to, developmental delay, autism, down syndrome, cerebral palsy, and much more. OTs evaluate patients using clinical reasoning and standardized assessments in order to create treatment plans that help children participate in activities they want, need, and have to do in every day life. Children's main occupation is often school, making the focus of OT the development of children's fine motor, visual motor, and visual perceptual skills needed to participate in school tasks. Intervention is provided in a play based manner for optimal skill development.

Keywords:

Fine Motor Skills: The ability to make movements utilizing the small muscles of your hands. This skill is needed for grasping a writing utensil, writing neatly on the lines, buttoning buttons, and much more.

Visual Motor Skills: The ability to interpret visual information and respond with a motor action. This skill is needed for skills such as writing/copying letters, getting food onto a fork, hitting a ball with a baseball bat, and much more.

Visual Perceptual Skills: The brain's ability to interpret what the eye sees. This skill is important for activities like writing, dressing, playing and much more.

These activities are not therapeutic interventions and do not substitute for therapeutic intervention.

How many of each ice cream can you find?

Color and count!

Cut, color, and glue to make an ice
cream cone!

 # Cut, color, and glue to make an ice cream cone!

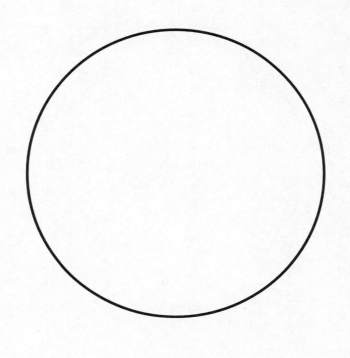

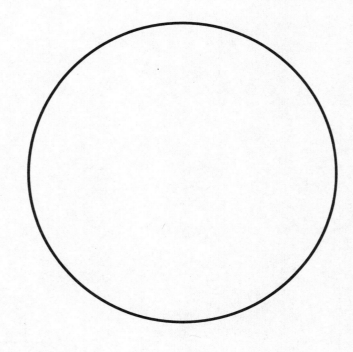

Count how many ice cream scoops are on each cone. Write the number in the box.

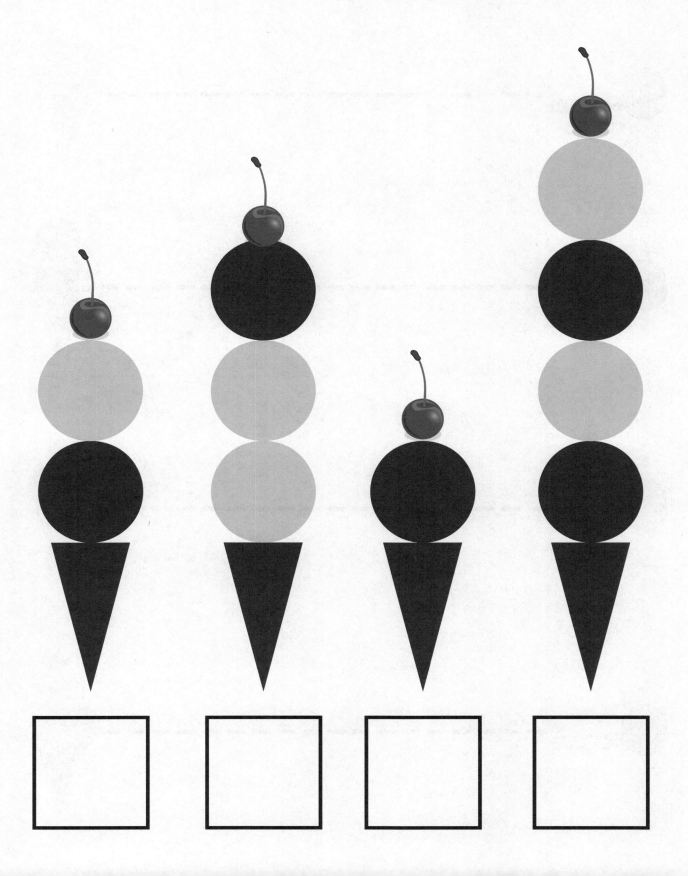

Trace the lines to get to the ice cream.

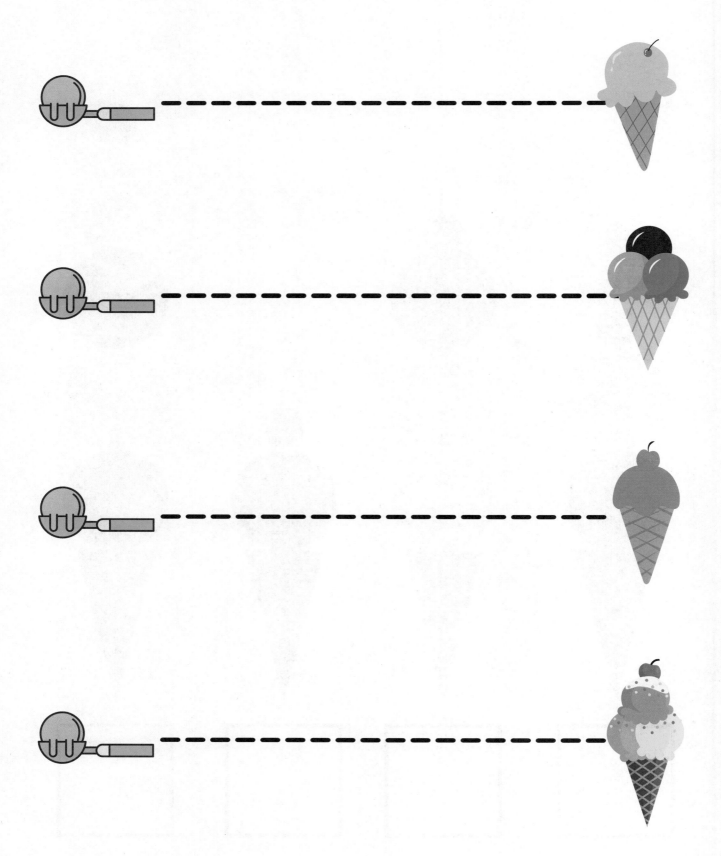

Trace the lines to get to the ice cream.

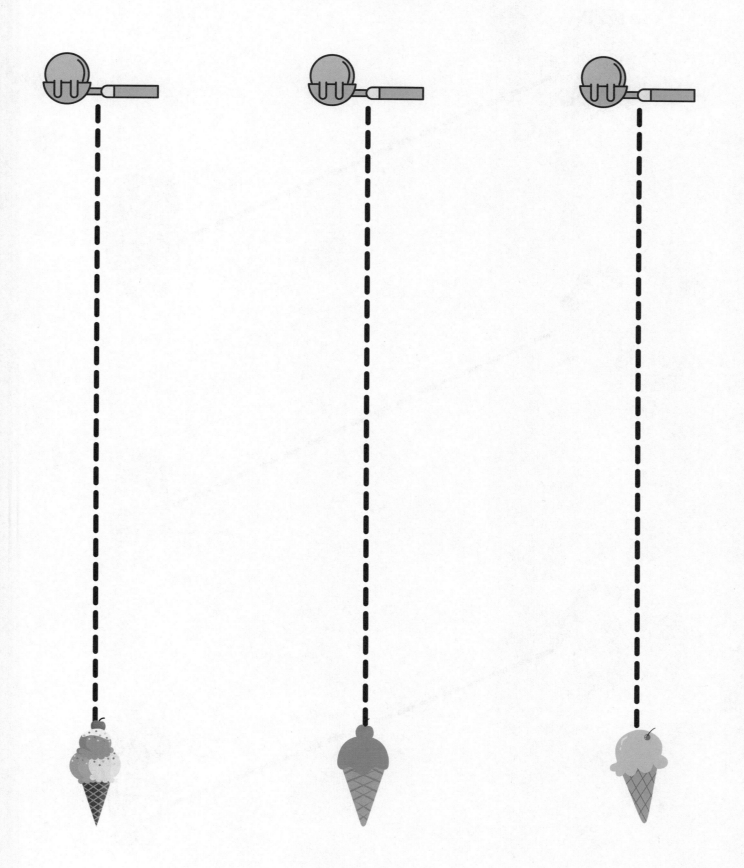

Trace the lines to get to the ice cream.

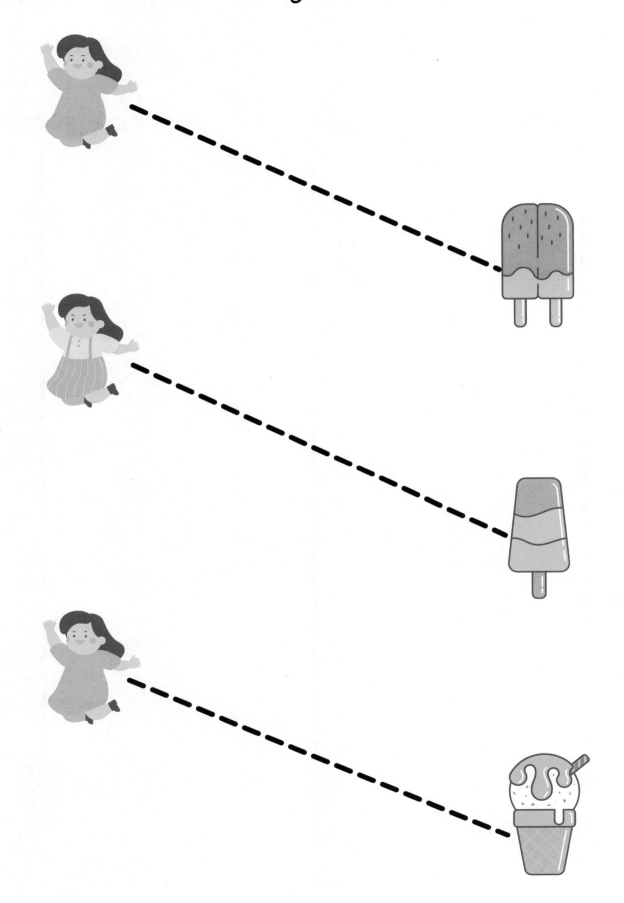

Trace the lines to get to the ice cream.

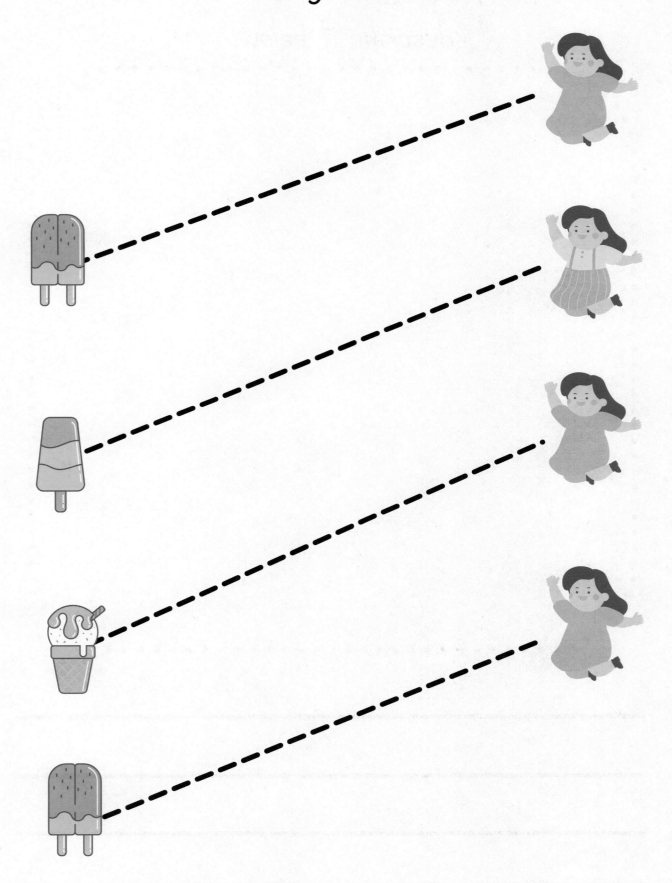

Draw a picture of your favorite ice cream and describe it below!

_____

_____

_____

_____

Complete the Pattern

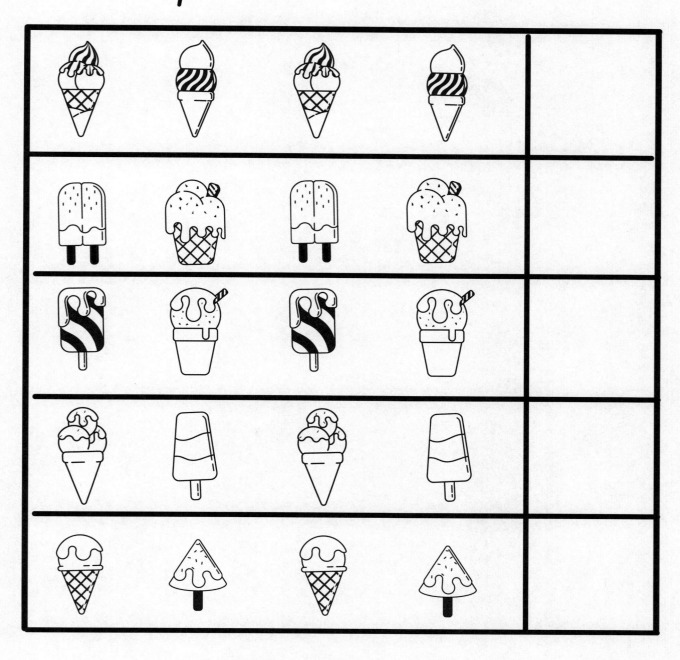

COLOR, CUT & GLUE

Color in the stripes to make a rainbow.

Draw lines to match the colors.

 PURPLE

 BLUE

 RED

 ORANGE

 GREEN

 YELLOW

Write a word that begins with each
letter of the word "Rainbow".

R _____

A _____

I _____

N _____

B _____

O _____

W _____

Write the words in the correct boxes:

Orange   Green   Yellow   Blue

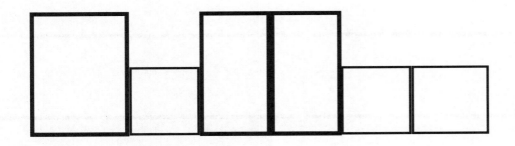

 # Draw Your Own Rainbow

Write about a time you saw a rainbow!

_____

_____

_____

_____

_____

Color in the circles to make a rainbow.

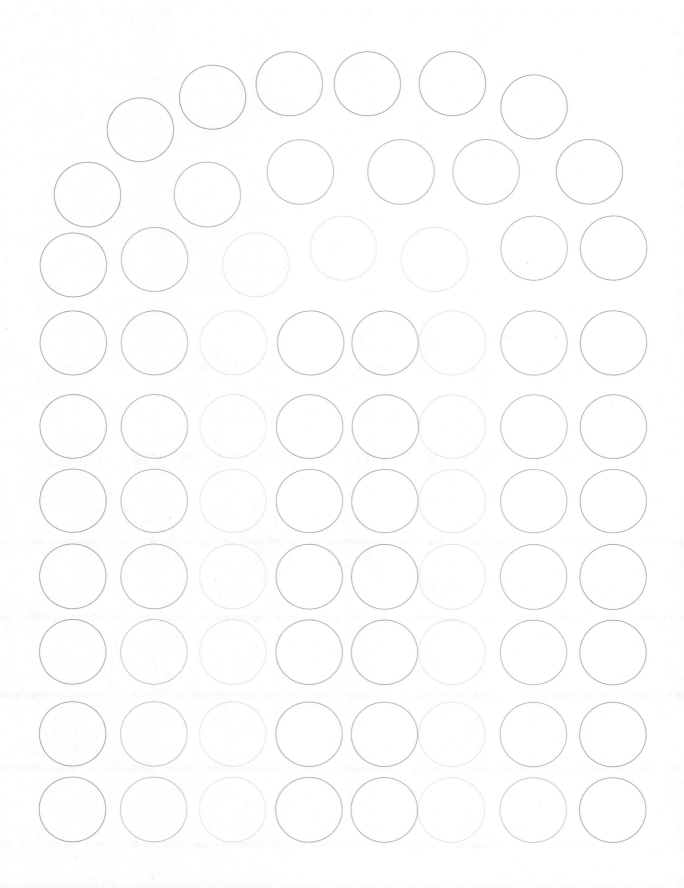

Draw lines to match the animals.

Trace the names of the animals.

Help the koala get to the tree to take a nap.
Take your time and stay inside the lines.

How many of each animal can you find?

BIG   SMALL

Which animals are big and which are small? Cut and Sort!

Write the words in the correct boxes:

Monkey   Frog   Mouse   Giraffe

Trace the Shapes.

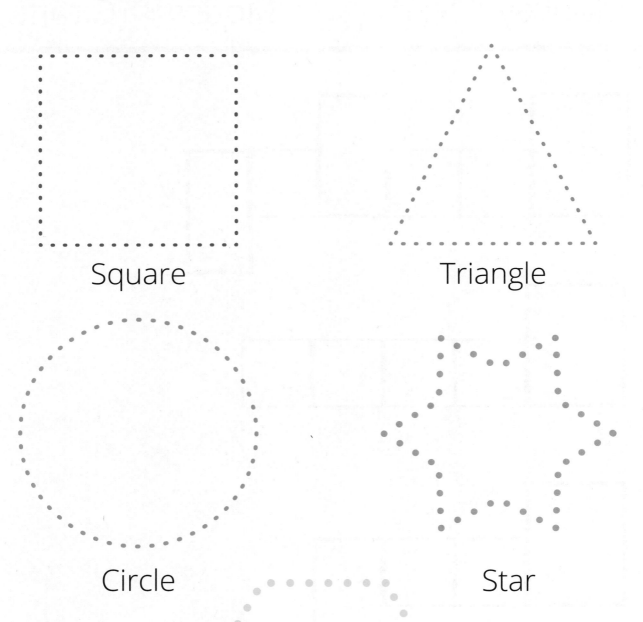

Square

Triangle

Circle

Star

Hexagon

Trace the Words.

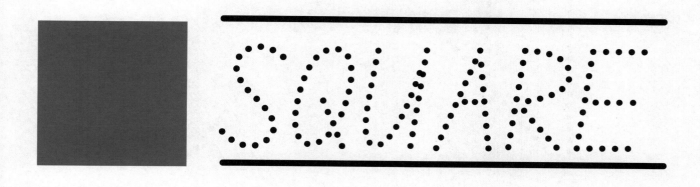

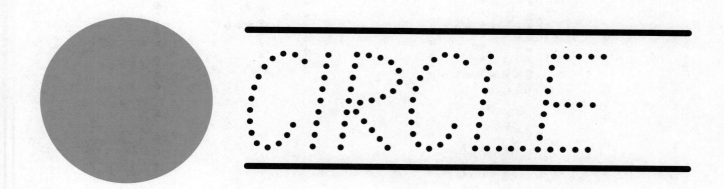

Trace the lines to draw a house.

Write the words in the correct boxes:

Circle   Square   Diamond   Triangle

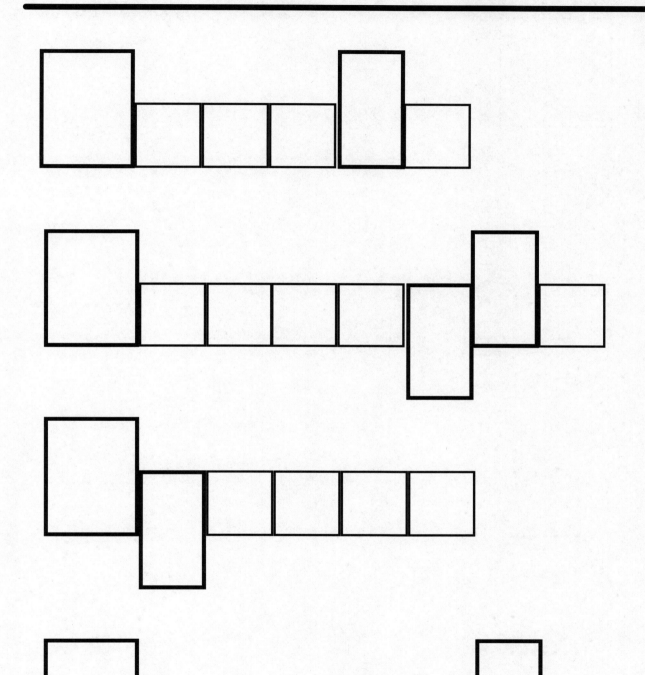

Color in the shapes, then draw lines to match them.

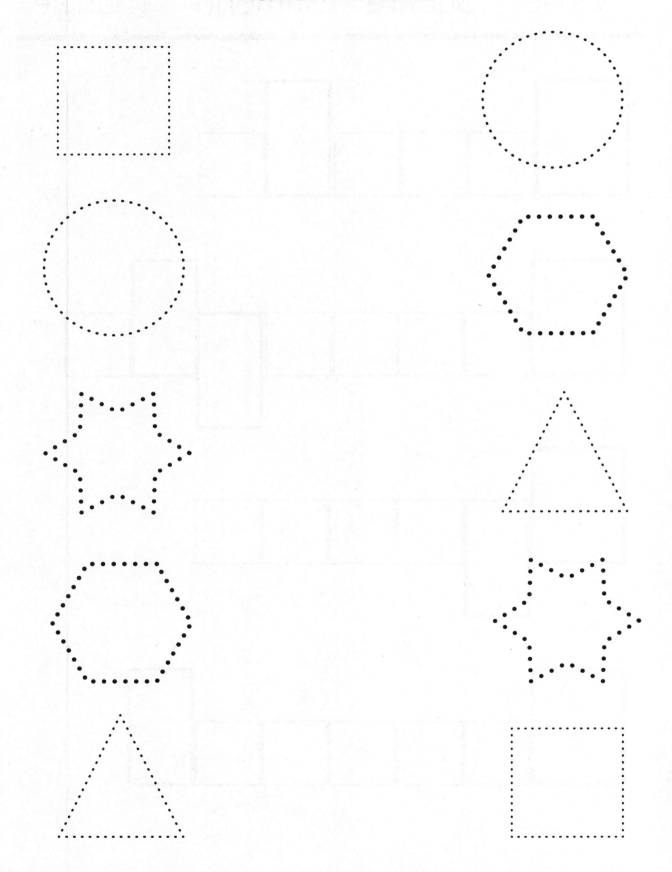

Connect the dots to copy the patterns.

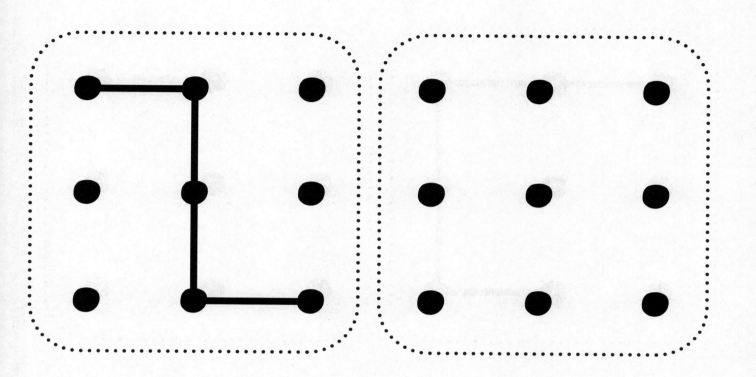

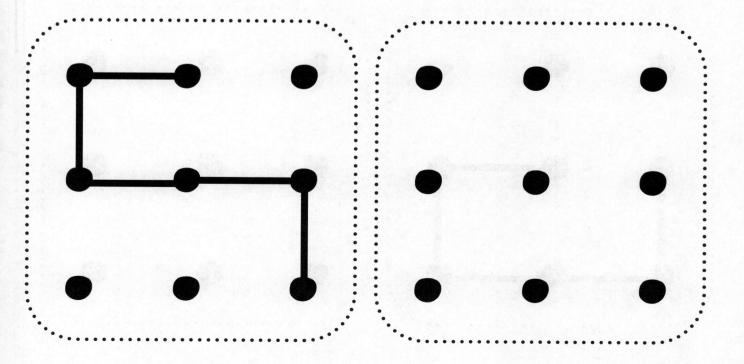

Connect the dots to copy the patterns.

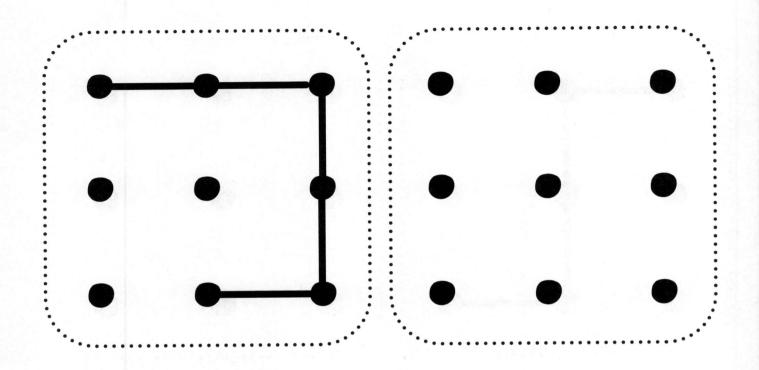

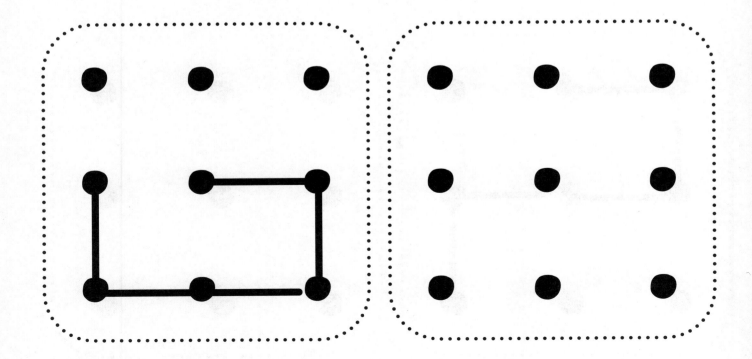

Draw the shapes in the matching boxes.

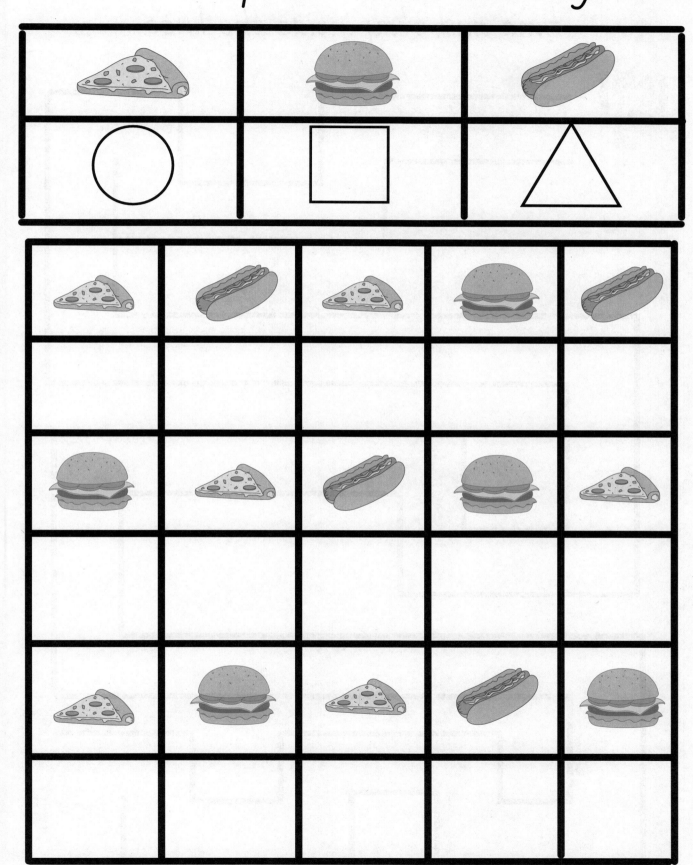

Help the child get to their snack! Take your time and stay inside the lines.

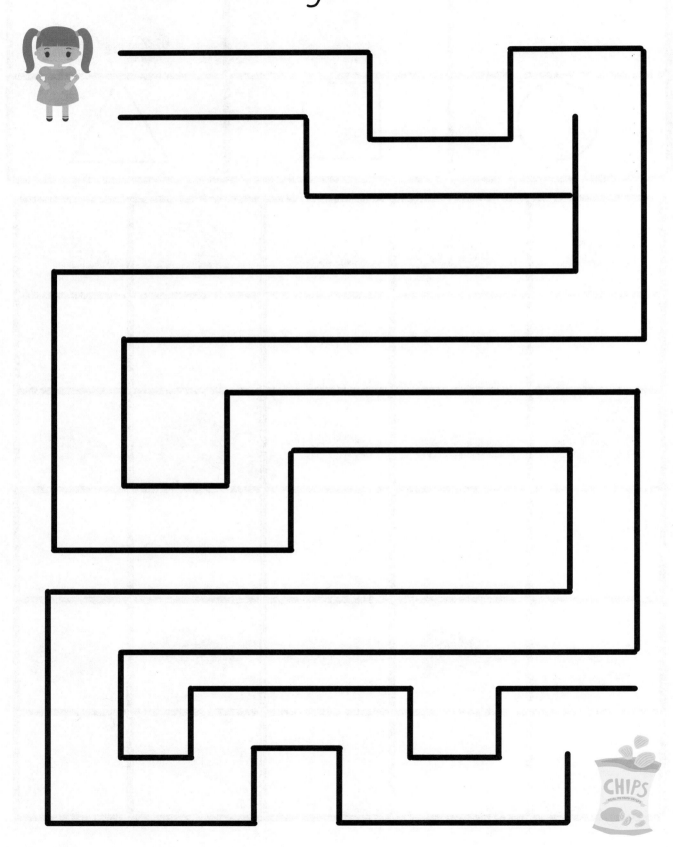

Write the words in the correct boxes:

Burger   Fries   Chips   Hotdog

Draw lines to match the food.

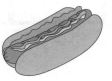

Cut out the items and glue them together to make a sandwich!

Cut out the items and glue them together to make a sandwich!

Cut out the items and glue them together to make a sandwich!

How many of each food can you find?

Draw a picture of your favorite food! Describe it below.

_____

_____

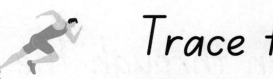 # Trace the balls.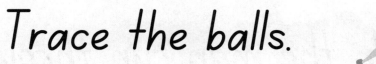

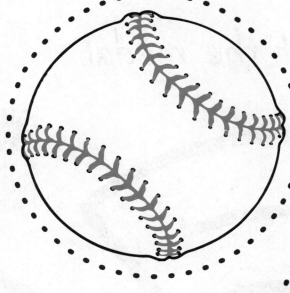

Help the man run through the maze to get the medal.

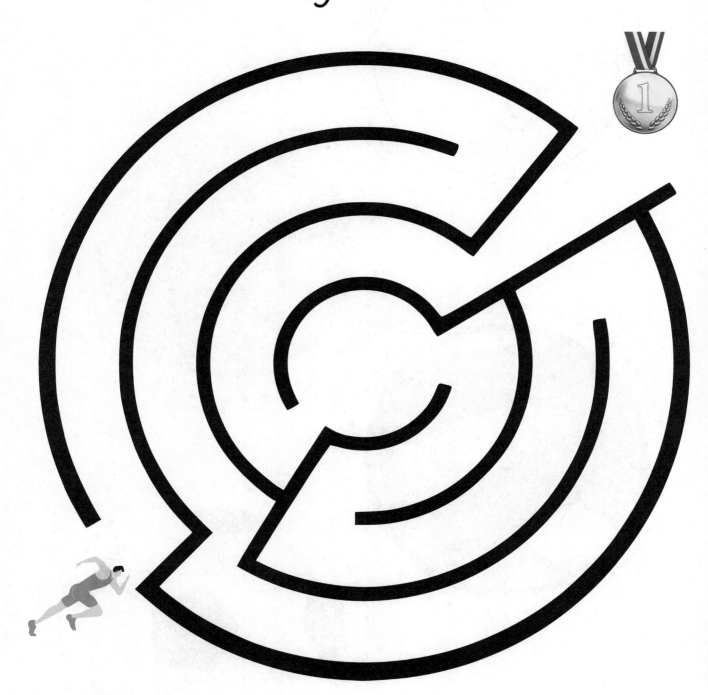

Trace the words.

 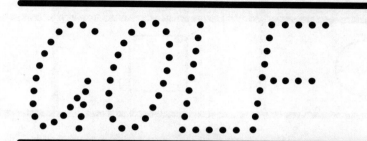

 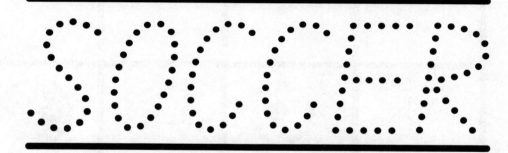

 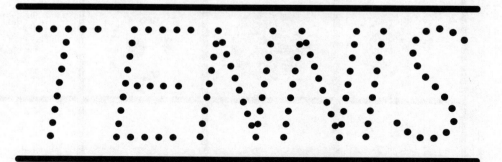

Draw the shapes in the matching boxes.

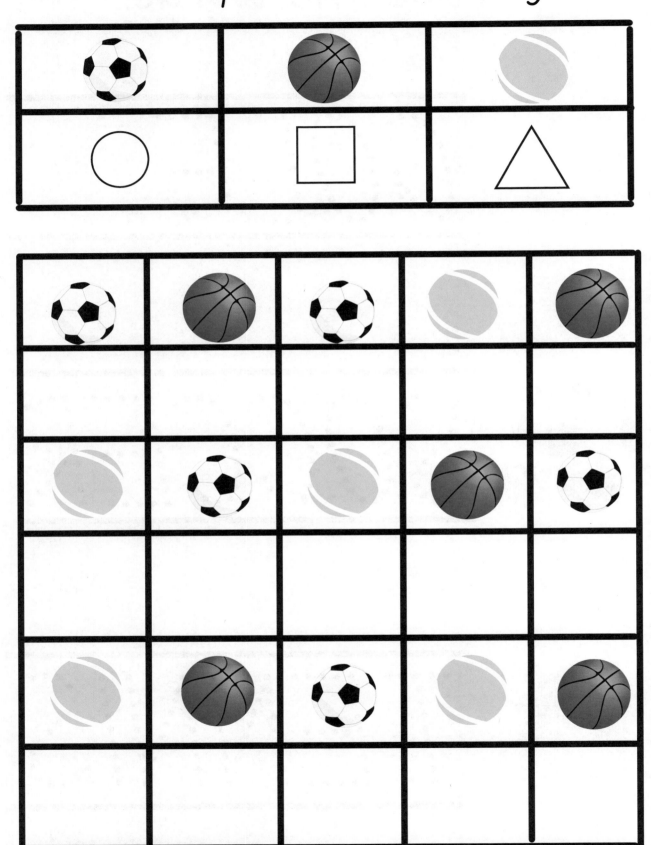

Trace the lines to get the ball to the goal!

Draw a line through the obstacle to score a goal!

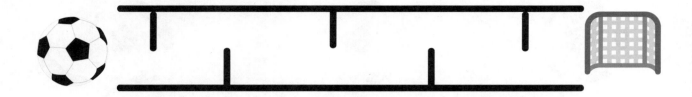

Trace the line to score a basket!

Trace the line to throw the baseball to the mitt!

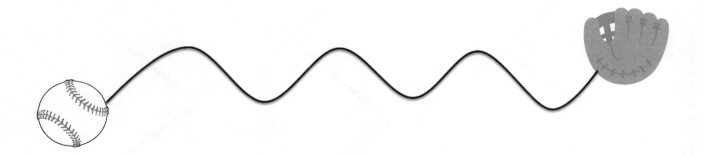

Color in the circles to score a hole-in-one!

Complete the Pattern.

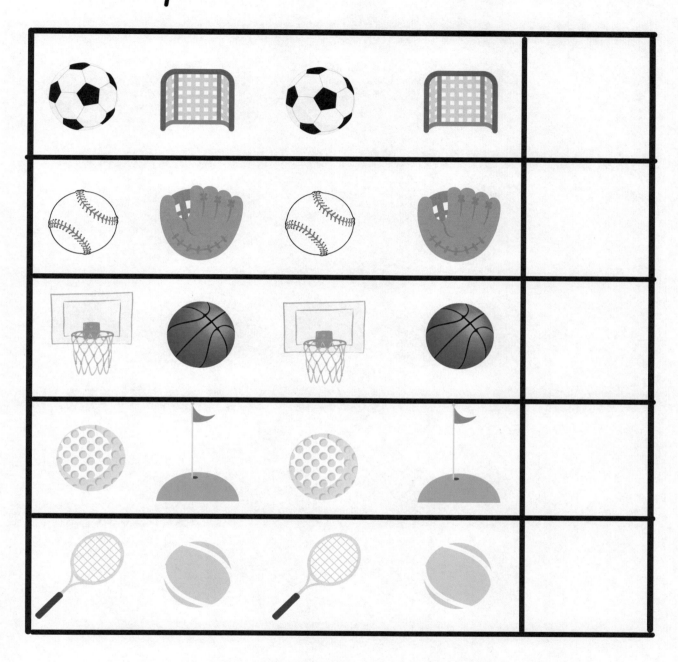

COLOR, CUT & PASTE

Write in the missing first letter.

| | O | C | C | E | R |

| | O | L | F |

| | E | N | N | I | S |

Trace the lines.

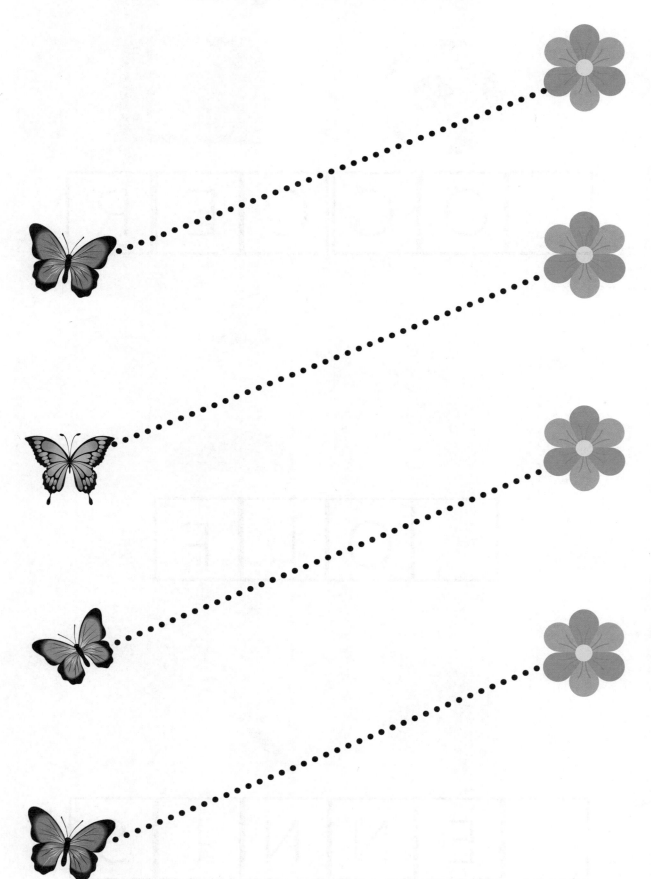

Trace the lines.

Trace the lines.

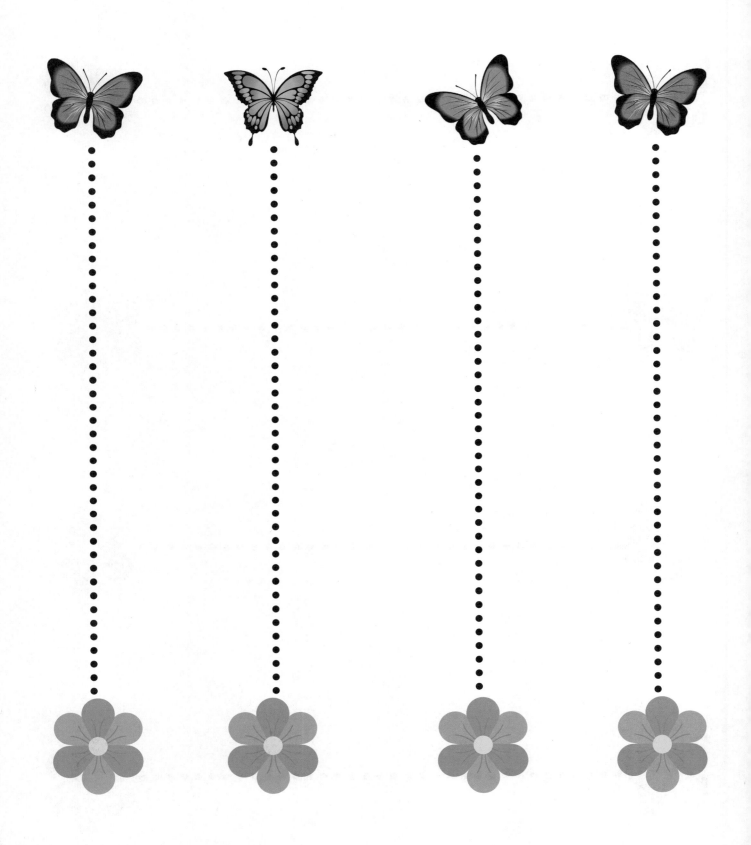

Pink   Blue

Which butterflies are pink and which are

blue? Cut and Sort!

Cut on the lines to reach the flowers.

Color the butterflies.

Write the words in the correct boxes:

Butterfly   Spring   Garden   Flower

Trace the letters.

Draw lines to match the letter to the picture that starts with the same sound.

A

K

Z

D

B
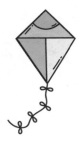

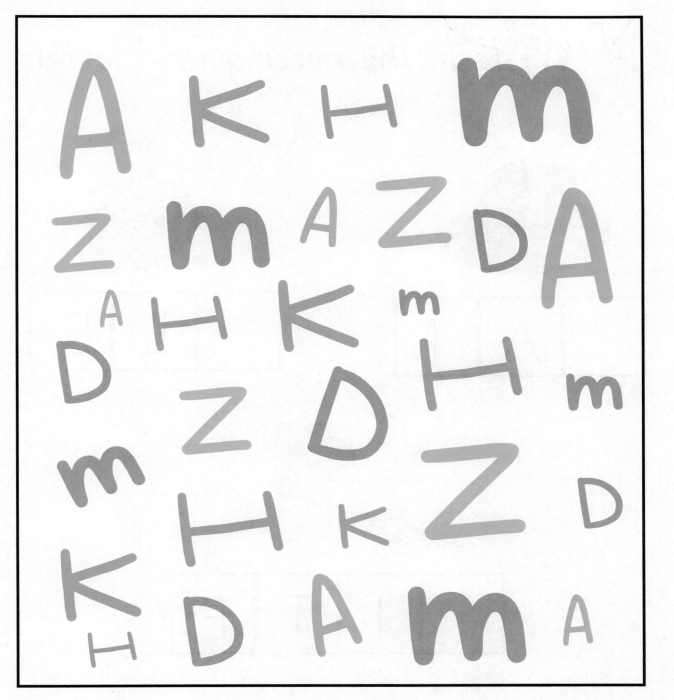

How many of each letter can you find?

A _____   m _____   K _____

Z _____   H _____   D _____

Write in the missing first letter.

| | A | T |

| | E | E |

| | I | T | E |

| | O | G |

| | A | T |

Color in the circles to make letter "A".

Color in all the circles with the letter "A" or "a".

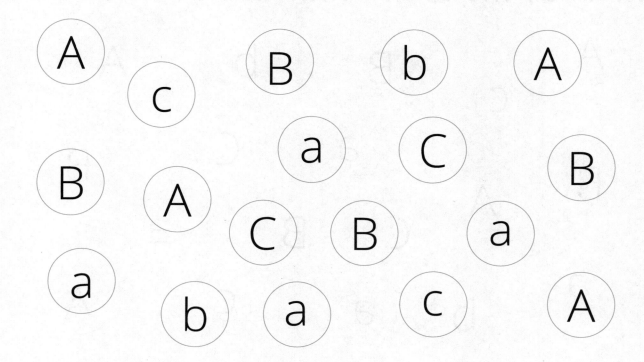

Color in the circles to make letter "B".

Color in all the circles with the letter "B" or "b".

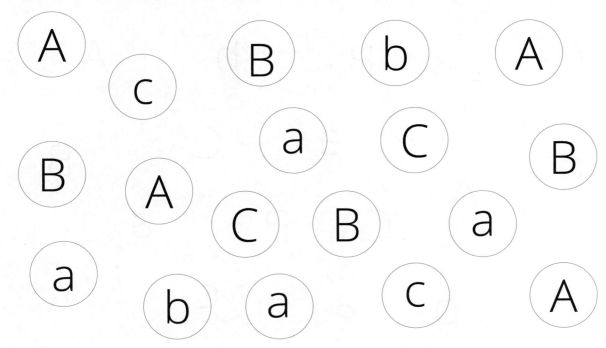

Color in the circles to make letter "C".

Color in all the circles with the letter "C" or "c".

About the Author

Grace Scorzetti MS OTR/L has been working as a pediatric occupational therapist for over five years helping children with a variety of needs participate in their valued activities. She was inspired to create this book after hearing parents ask for simple, fun, OT activities that could be done at home. Grace is also the creator "FUNctional Play" kits. The kits are designed to help kids develop skills needed for school tasks, dressing, eating, grooming etc. in a play-based manner. Her "FUNctional Play" kits can be found on her Instagram @functionalot.

A Note from the Author

I hope you find the activities in this book fun and helpful. I thoroughly enjoyed creating these activities for your kiddos, and often use them in my own OT practice!

45540629R00041